Shy Shark

Story by Michaela Morgan
Pictures by Elena Gomez

OXFORD
UNIVERSITY PRESS

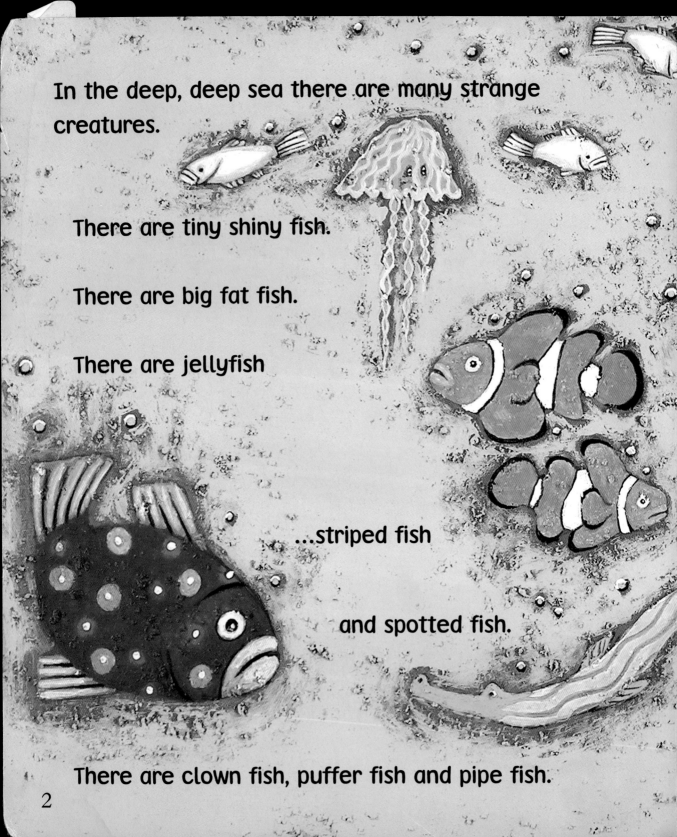

In the deep, deep sea there are many strange creatures.

There are tiny shiny fish.

There are big fat fish.

There are jellyfish

...striped fish

and spotted fish.

There are clown fish, puffer fish and pipe fish.

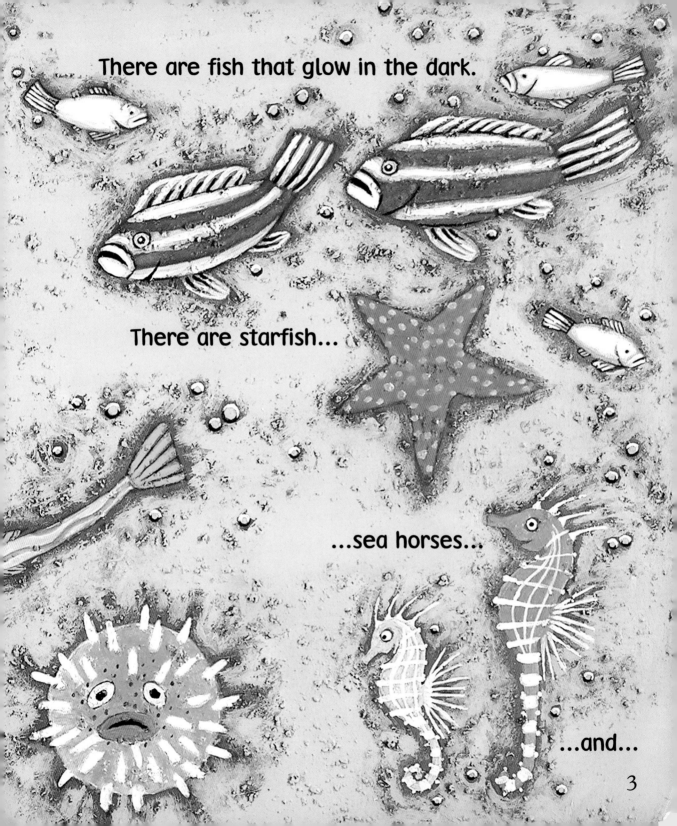

There are fish that glow in the dark.

There are starfish...

...sea horses...

...and...

3

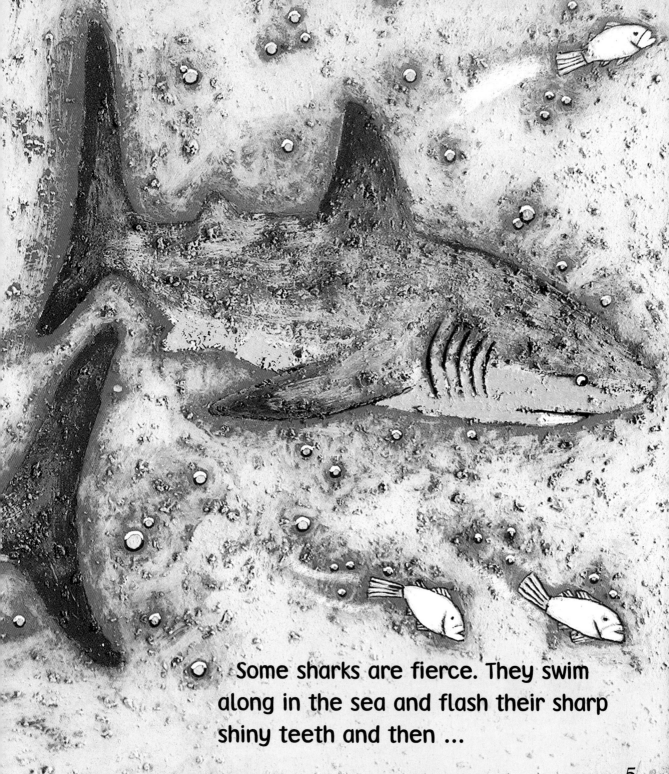

Some sharks are fierce. They swim along in the sea and flash their sharp shiny teeth and then ...

5

...they...

SNAP!

That is why many of
the sea creatures stay away
from sharks. And that is why one little
shark was very lonely.

This little shark was not fierce
at all. He was frightened of some
of the other sharks and he was shy.
Everyone called him Shy Shark.

He lay in the shadows and watched
the other creatures. He wished he
could be friends with them.
But when he swam
up to them...

Whoosh!

...with a flurry
of fins, they all swam away.
They didn't want to be snapped up by a shark.

7

So Shy Shark was lonely and sad.

He wished he could dash and dart about with the tiny, shiny fish. He wanted to joke with the jelly fish.

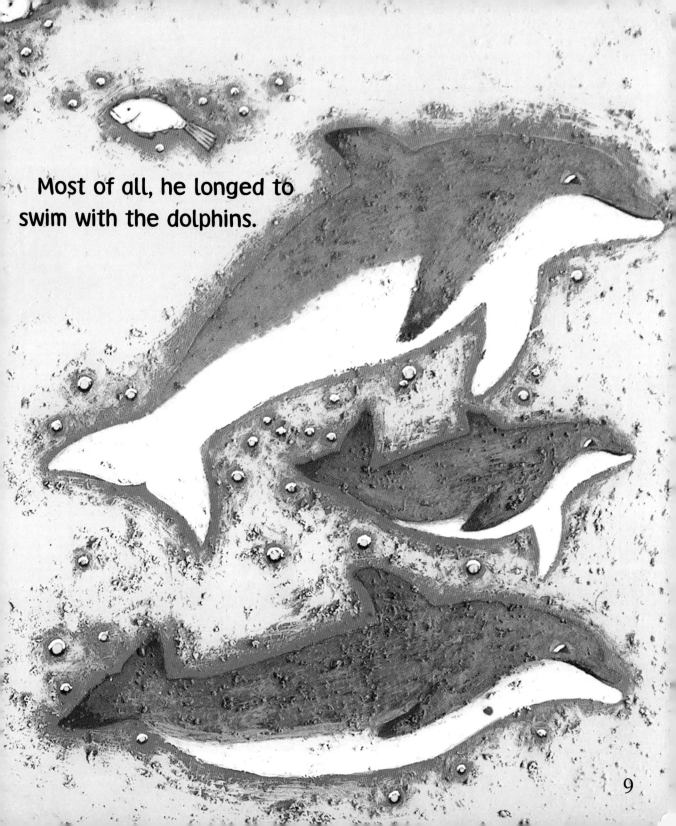

Most of all, he longed to
swim with the dolphins.

9

The dolphins always had lots of fun. They swam fast and they jumped high. They shone in the sunlight and they always seemed to be smiling and happy.

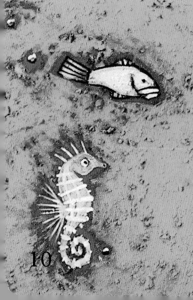

"I want to play," whispered Shy Shark, but nobody heard him.

11

One day, everyone in the sea was
swimming and playing. Shy Shark
hid in the shadows and watched them.

He saw the tiny, shiny fish playing tig.

He looked at the seahorses
racing each other.

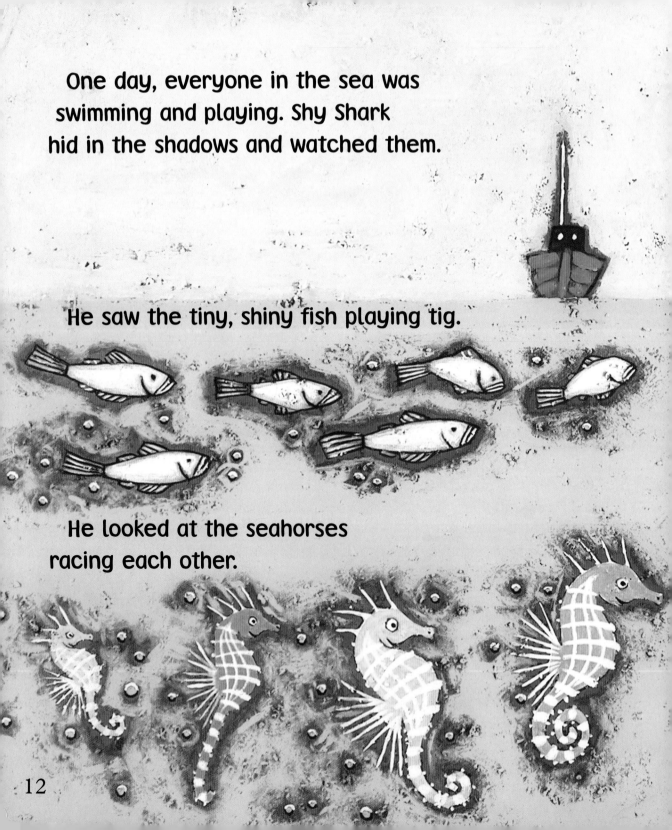

He gazed at the dolphins skimming
high in the water and leaping
up to the sun.

Then Shy Shark saw something else!

He saw a dark, dark shadow
coming over the sea.
It was a fishing boat.

Suddenly …

Whoosh!

… a net was thrown down.

All the sea creatures were trapped in the net.

Some of the tiny, shiny fish slipped
out of the net, but the larger
creatures were trapped.
The big, fat fish
were trapped.
The jellyfish
and the starfish,
the striped fish
and the
spotted fish ...

... the clown fish,
the puffer fish
and the pipe fish
were all trapped ...
... and so were the dolphins.
Three big dolphins were trapped tight in the net.

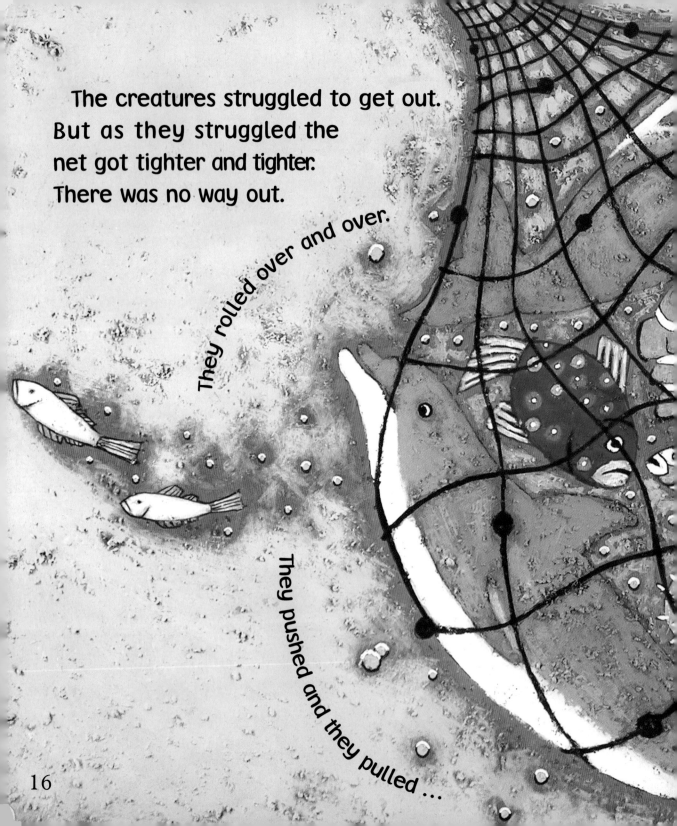

The creatures struggled to get out.
But as they struggled the
net got tighter and tighter.
There was no way out.

They rolled over and over.

They pushed and they pulled ...

16

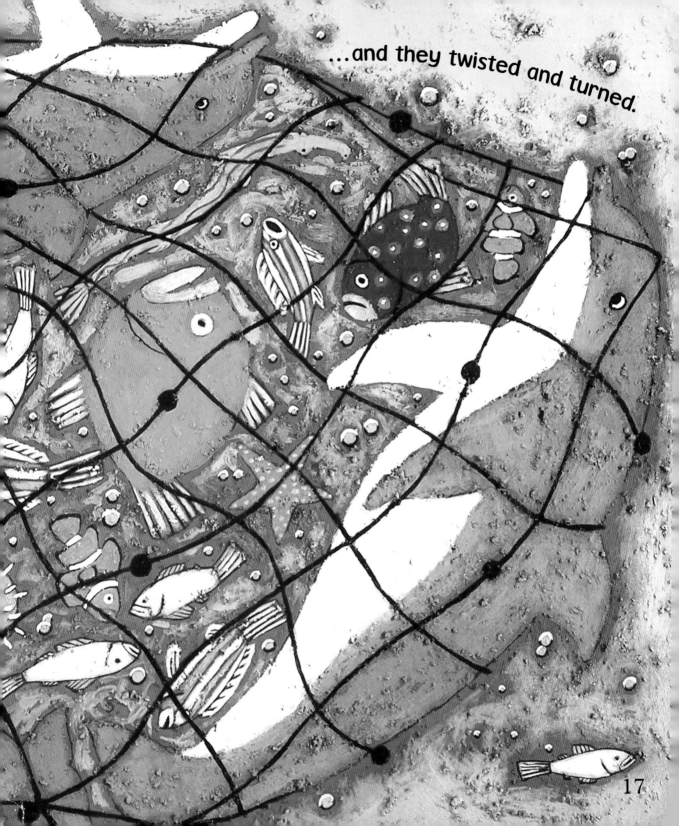

...and they twisted and turned.

17

Then Shy Shark had an idea!

He swam out of the shadows and went right up to the net.

Inside the net, all the fish and the dolphins were shaking with fear.
"Oh no!" they thought. "We can't get away from that shark with big, sharp teeth."

Shy Shark swam right up to the net.
With a **SNAP** he bit right through it.

SNAP!

20

All the fish and the dolphins tumbled out.
In a flash of fins, they all swam away to safety.
Shy Shark watched them go.
"Goodbye," he said, but nobody heard him.
He felt very lonely again.

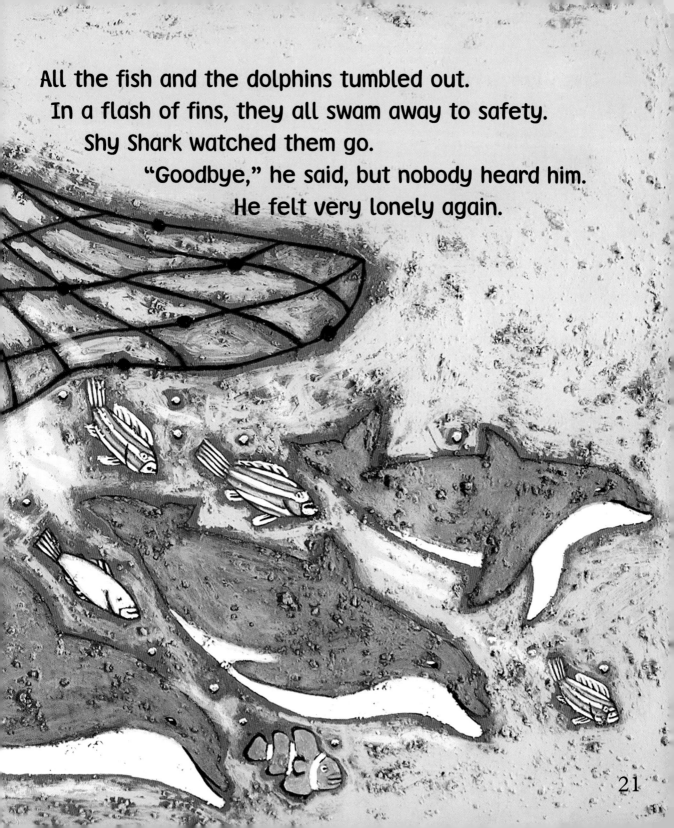

Then the three big dolphins swam towards him. Dolphins are very brave creatures. They came very close to Shy Shark.

"We want to say thank you," the first dolphin said. "Please tell us how we can repay you," said the second dolphin.

"Thank you," said Shy Shark. "There is something I want. I would really like to swim with you sometimes." "Of course!" said the third dolphin. And all the dolphins smiled.

You can still see all sorts of creatures in the sea.
There are tiny shiny fish, big fat fish, all sorts of
fish. And there are dolphins.

They leap and shine and smile in the sun.

If you look very carefully you will see one
very happy little shark swimming with them.

Shy Shark's wish has come true!